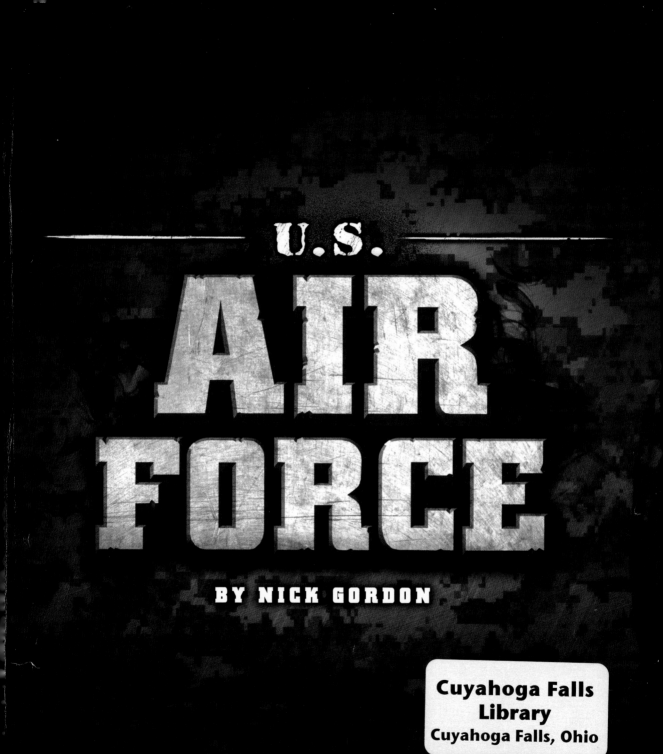

U.S. AIR FORCE

BY NICK GORDON

BELLWETHER MEDIA · MINNEAPOLIS, MN

EPIC BOOKS are no ordinary books. They burst with intense action, high-speed heroics, and shadows of the unknown. Are you ready for an Epic adventure?

This edition first published in 2013 by Bellwether Media, Inc.

No part of this publication may be reproduced in whole or in part without written permission of the publisher. For information regarding permission, write to Bellwether Media, Inc., Attention: Permissions Department, 5357 Penn Avenue South, Minneapolis, MN 55419.

Library of Congress Cataloging-in-Publication Data

Gordon, Nick.
U.S. Air Force / by Nick Gordon.
    p. cm. (Epic books: U.S. military)
Includes bibliographical references and index.
    Summary: "Engaging images accompany information about the U.S. Air Force. The combination of high-interest subject matter and light text is intended for students in grades 2 through 7"–Provided by publisher.
    Audience: Ages 6-12.
    ISBN 978-1-60014-826-2 (hbk. : alk. paper)
    1. United States. Air Force–Juvenile literature. I. Title.
    UG633.G627 2013
    358.400973–dc23   2012008561

Printed in the United States of America, North Mankato, MN.

TABLE OF CONTENTS

THE U.S. AIR FORCE

The United States Air Force is a branch of the **United States Armed Forces**. Its main job is **aerial warfare**.

UNITED STATES AIR FORCE

Founded: 1947

Headquarters: Arlington, Virginia

Motto: "Aim High ... Fly-Fight-Win"

Size: More than 300,000 active personnel

Major Engagements: Korean War, Vietnam War, Gulf War, Afghanistan War, Iraq War, War on Terror

Air Force pilots fly airplanes and helicopters. Other members of the Air Force support the pilots. Mechanics fix aircraft. Air traffic controllers tell pilots when to take off and land.

Capt Brett "Mace" Swiger

RESCUE

AIR FORCE VEHICLES

F-22 RAPTOR

The Air Force uses many kinds of aircraft. Fighter planes attack targets. The F-22 Raptor has **stealth** technology. This hides it from enemy **radar**.

The B-2 Spirit and other bombers attack targets on the ground. They drop bombs from high in the sky.

B-2 SPIRIT

Spy planes gather **intelligence**.
The MQ-9 Reaper is a **drone**.
It can spy on or attack enemies.

MQ-9 REAPER

U-2 SPY PLANE

AIR FORCE FACT

The U-2 spy plane flies above 70,000 feet (21,335 meters). This is too high for radar to find it.

HH-60 PAVE HAWK

The Air Force also uses larger planes and helicopters. The C-5 Galaxy and HH-60 Pave Hawk transport **cargo** and troops.

AIR FORCE FACT

The C-5 Galaxy opens at both the front and rear. It can be loaded and unloaded on either end.

C-5 GALAXY

AIR FORCE MISSIONS

The Air Force performs many **missions**. It bombs enemy bases and attacks enemy aircraft.

AIR FORCE FACT

The Air Force delivers supplies to those in need. Often the supplies parachute out of airplanes!

The Air Force also gathers information. Spy planes take pictures of enemy territory. Pilots watch for enemy troops and weapons.

PILOT

Members of the Air Force also perform **search-and-rescue** missions. They find people who are lost or in trouble. This is one of the many ways they serve the people of the United States.

466

6466

GLOSSARY

aerial warfare—military operations that involve aircraft

cargo—supplies, such as food, equipment, and weapons

drone—an aircraft controlled by remote control

intelligence—information about an enemy

missions—military tasks

radar—a system that uses radio waves to locate targets

search-and-rescue—a mission in which someone in a dangerous situation is brought to safety

stealth—an aircraft's ability to fly without being spotted by radar

United States Armed Forces—the five branches of the United States military; they are the Air Force, the Army, the Coast Guard, the Marine Corps, and the Navy.

TO LEARN MORE

At the Library

Doeden, Matt. *The U.S. Air Force.* Mankato, Minn.: Capstone Press, 2009.

White, Steve. *Combat Fighter: F-22 Raptor.* New York, N.Y.: Children's Press, 2007.

Zobel, Derek. *United States Air Force.* Minneapolis, Minn.: Bellwether Media, 2008.

On the Web

Learning more about the U.S. Air Force is as easy as 1, 2, 3.

1. Go to www.factsurfer.com.

2. Enter "U.S. Air Force" into the search box.

3. Click the "Surf" button and you will see a list of related Web sites.

With factsurfer.com, finding more information is just a click away.

INDEX